7

RULES TO INFLUENCE BEHAVIOUR AND WIN AT CYBER SECURITY AWARENESS

For my father, Deepak, who made me the man I am today. For my wife, Urvi, without whose love and support this book wouldn't be possible. For my mother, Hema, my brother, Sunny, and sister-in-law, Sharada, whose encouragement and enthusiasm keep me going. For my grandparents, whom I can never thank enough for everything they sacrificed for me.

A special thanks to Dan Jones for his mentorship and to Paul De Araujo and Sameer Karamchandani for their friendship and support of this book.

7 RULES TO INFLUENCE BEHAVIOUR AND WIN AT CYBER SECURITY AWARENESS

Table of Contents

1   What Will This Book Do for You?

- If you're new to cyber security, it will help you understand and communicate the topic better. It will also give you a clear, jargon-free action plan and resources to jump-start your own security awareness efforts.

- If you're an experienced cyber security professional, it will challenge your existing assumptions and provide a better way to increase the effectiveness of your cyber awareness programs.

- It will empower you to influence user behaviour and subsequently reduce cyber incidents caused by the human factor.

- It will enable you to avoid common mistakes that make cyber security awareness programs ineffective.

- It will help make you a more engaging leader and presenter.

- Most importantly, it won't waste your time with boring content (yes, that's one of the rules!).

2   Introduction

I distinctly remember the scene like it happened yesterday, although it has been a few years now. I walked into a room full of mostly hard-nosed, seasoned, technical IT professionals where I was invited to speak on the importance of following good security processes and standards. I know the topic sounds boring—it is quite dry, and presenting it to a group of people who probably have heard it all before made it even more challenging. This was aggravated by the fact that technical IT people generally have a low opinion of management types in suits telling them how to do their jobs better. In their minds, they feel these people don't have a true understanding of their roles and day-to-day challenges they face.

However, the good news for me is that I like tough environments. There are very few things that match the thrill that comes with winning over a difficult crowd through your public speaking and presentations. Also, I was determined to make my presentation useful to the audience, and thereby ensure the teachings from it had a higher likelihood of being applied.

Now, a lot of IT personnel are familiar with the negative connotations associated with use of the word "cowboy" in their job's context. This word implies a cavalier attitude towards following established standards and processes and bypassing them in order to get their jobs done faster. From personal experience working with numerous IT teams over the years, I know they don't like this description of them. In their minds, they are doing the best they can under the circumstances, which can include aggressive and urgent timelines to deliver outcomes, often with limited resources.

To get attention and engagement from this tough crowd, I started my presentation with a real-life picture of me from Facebook wearing a cowboy hat, boots, and singing karaoke to Johnny Cash's classics. Being an avid country music fan and a pretty good country dancer, if I do say so myself, I have lots of such stories and pictures. Starting my presentation with that image and implying, tongue in cheek, that I am one of the "cowboys" got a lot of chuckles from the attendees and instantly eased the atmosphere in the room. I followed that up with my customary introductory slide that had my name and senior cyber security job title, accompanied by a lot of initials that indicate the various industry certifications I hold. I then made a comment with a slightly sarcastic smile on my face: "Hope you understand that my title and all the initials following it just mean I'm a really smart guy."

The way I said it made the audience start laughing. They knew I wasn't going to be just another cyber presenter in a suit and that I was willing to make light of all the assumed self-importance of senior leaders who think they are automatically owed respect due to their titles and qualifications. From there on, it was easy. I had the audience interested, engaged, and totally involved with my overall message on security processes and standards. In fact, I had several audience members walk up to me after the presentation to say how much they'd enjoyed the talk and discussed ways in which they'd apply the principles I shared. All said and done, I consider this presentation a success!

Now, this wasn't the first time I had adopted a laid-back and humorous approach tailored for the audience in the room. All through my years doing public speaking and presentations on cyber security, I have used similar tailored approaches, be it presenting to a group of accountants in Colorado, USA or to a group of executives at a conference in Sydney, Australia.

At a high level, my approach to awareness is all about knowing what to communicate, how to communicate, who to communicate to, and when to communicate. Over my career, I'm fortunate to have had the opportunity to work with people in different countries with various backgrounds. Through my years of professional experience, public presentations, and learning from both successes and failures, I have perfected a process that works effectively for creating winning cyber security awareness programs.

Now let's look at some points that make a strong case on the need for cyber security awareness. On a nearly daily basis, when you read news about cyber-attacks—causing millions of personal records to be leaked, businesses to suffer crippling damages to their systems, or countries to target each other in cyber space—we start imagining sophisticated hackers and these really smart people who can just break into our computers and smart devices as they please. There's nothing much we can do, right?

Not so fast.

If you study credible public reports and expert analysis on cyber security incidents, you'll discover this startling fact. Most cyber security incidents— approximately seven out of ten—occur due to human errors and behaviours, not complicated technical attacks. Again, let that number sink in—*seven* out of ten! Even most of the attacks that are described as "sophisticated" end up having human mistakes, such as falling for phishing attacks, at their core. Cyber security, then, is fundamentally a human issue, not a technology issue. Thus, it requires a process of communication that is focused on connecting and resonating with humans.

I wrote this book to share my process with you. The reason I want to share a process that actually works is because of this important observation—most programs, campaigns, and efforts aimed at creating awareness on cyber security issues are failures. These programs have operated without a clear sense of good objectives, and thanks to their boring, inconsistent, and overwhelmingly negative approaches, they have succeeded in scaring their audiences into inaction and, sadly, attitudes of apathy. They have been unsuccessful at the one thing all awareness campaigns intend to do—influence user behaviour.

I also wrote this book to challenge the traditional thinking behind current cyber security communication efforts and provide an actionable set of rules for doing it better. To make my rules more credible and authoritative, I have incorporated relevant research and proven teachings from outside the traditional cyber areas, such as behavioural psychology, neuroscience, and public health campaigns. Additionally, I have also drawn wisdom from several global bodies of knowledge in the technology domain, backed by my own real-world experience of building successful cyber awareness and training programs across multiple industry verticals. Applying these rules has enabled me to successfully train audiences from very different professional backgrounds, such as finance, energy, higher education, and healthcare. They have also enabled me to become an established cyber security speaker with presentations at leading national, regional, and local conferences. Simply put, these rules work. These rules show results.

I love this quote by Albert Einstein—"If you can't explain it simply, you don't understand it well enough." Far too often, books on cyber security or cyber risk come across as these thick textbook types, with most claiming to be definitive guides on the subject. While I think they do an average job of explaining cyber security concepts, I must admit they do a *brilliant* job of making it completely uninteresting to a non-techie who just wants to know more about the subject. They do this through a time-tested way of making things boring—extremely long books filled with academic writing, complete with unintelligible jargon and a lot of charts thrown in for added effect. If you prefer that type of work, I understand—but this book is not that.

This book is not a white paper or a research journal or a textbook. This is a cyber security book that is intended to be informative, while still being brief and humorous. It most certainly does not rely on boring hoodie-wearing hacker imagery, unnecessary hype, scary numbers, or jargon. The specific focus of this book is to provide no-nonsense, actionable advice on communicating cyber security awareness in a manner that influences user behaviour and shows results.

This book is for everyone regardless of their prior cyber security experience. This includes cyber security and IT professionals, consultants, change managers, communication specialists, senior executives, and people who are new to the world of cyber security.

Drawing inspiration from great leaders of the past and the success they had with communicating through their commandments and steps, I have communicated the content in this book through seven simple rules. Also, there is a resources section at the end of the book that contains a lot of useful information and links that'll help you with your cyber awareness efforts, as well enable you to learn more about other elements of cyber security. I'm aware this section may eventually become out of date, considering the rapid pace of change in the technology and cyber worlds. To address this, I strongly recommend you check the resources section on my website, https://www.chiragdjoshi.com, for regularly updated content. On a lighter note, you knew I had to mention my own website in my book. What public speaker and "expert" doesn't promote their own website, right?

Congratulations to you for taking a big step in the direction of communicating cyber security effectively by reading this book! How modest, but honest, of me to say that.

3   Cyber Security and the Human Factor

Before we get into cyber security awareness, let's look at the term "cyber security." This specific term went mainstream around 2014. I distinctly remember in the early 2000s that the common term was "IT Security," which then morphed into "Information Security." Many purists still debate the definitions and nuances of this topic—whether cyber security is a subset of information security, or if cyber security is a science with information security and IT security as its specific branches. However, for most people living in the real world, there is no true difference between these terms.

Keeping things straightforward—cyber security relates to the protection of information, systems, and devices, and by extension, people, and businesses that rely on them for their activities.

Just to make sure we're all on the same page when discussing cyber security awareness, let's revisit the general meaning of the term. Cyber security awareness is a broad term that encompasses a lot of different activities and mediums, such as face-to-face presentations, online training, websites, physical and digital posters, competitions, interactive forums, and so forth, with the goal to educate people on cyber threats and equip them to practice secure behaviour so as to minimize losses and disruptions caused by cyber incidents. Like all things in the modern world, it relies on a combination of people, processes, and technologies to achieve its objectives. In this book, I use the term "cyber security awareness program" to describe a formal set of activities that are run by an organization to train and educate its employees on cyber security.

The topics covered by cyber security awareness can include a host of different areas but typically include the following:

- How to protect yourself from scams and emails intended to trick you.
- How to protect against malware and viruses.
- How to protect your devices and information when traveling or working remotely.

- How to keep your devices updated and maintain backups.

- How to report suspicious cyber activities or incidents.

- How to meet expectations and policies regarding the use and management of information and IT systems.

Now in the introduction section of this book, we talked about how majority of cyber-attacks that are described as sophisticated still end up having human mistakes at their core.

As examples, let's look at separate cyber security breaches from 2019 impacting Wipro, an Indian IT outsourcing giant that provides services to some of the largest companies worldwide (Mendonca 2019), and Australian Catholic University, a major tertiary institution in Australia (Fellner 2019). These organizations are obviously very different in their functions. However, in both the cases, the primary cause of the incident was a successful phishing attack where their employees were tricked by malicious emails. There are dozens of such big-name examples that can be found through a quick Google search, but you get the point.

If you are not familiar with Phishing, it typically refers to nefarious emails that are designed to look like they're legitimate in source and intent. They'll often request you click on a link and provide valuable information, such as your social security number, bank account numbers, passwords, and credit card numbers. They may also prompt you to download an attachment or click on a link that is generally malicious in nature. It is important to note that phishing emails have gotten much smarter and harder to spot if you aren't paying close attention. Gone are the days when they were full of spelling mistakes and poor grammar, claiming to come from mysterious princes.

Why are humans targeted, you may ask? To answer that question, let's look at the world around us. Technology has fundamentally and irreversibly transformed our lives. We are now living in the digital age, where we can stream innumerable movies, shows, books, and music on-demand. We probably have enough content available on-demand that can last us for years if we do nothing but consume it 24/7. On average, we have around seventeen connected devices in our homes now! And this number is only increasing.

We live in a world where technology and the Internet of Things (IoT) have allowed amazing advances in human fitness, nutrition, medicine, and industrial production. IoT has a lot of technical definitions, but to make it simple, it refers to interconnected devices with on/off functionality that may use the internet to communicate with each other. These devices can make decisions and undertake actions by interacting with other devices or by sensing their own internal and external states, with or without human intervention. This definition typically excludes devices such as laptops but includes everything from movement and sleep trackers, wearables such as Google Glass and smart watches, to smart versions of appliances such as refrigerators, TVs, thermostats, lamps, washing machines, and so forth that can be controlled remotely. IoT also has applications in major diverse industries, including mining and agriculture.

Our collaboration and communication tools have made it possible for us to speak, work, and connect with people all over the world in an instant, with a cost that is a fraction of what it was as recently as a decade ago.

There is also an increasing convergence between the cyber and physical worlds. While this opens up lots of great opportunities in the areas of industrial automation, an unfortunate consequence is that things like bullying or harassment don't stop when you leave the school or city—they can reach you all the time through technology.

The primary driver of these trends is the rapid evolution of cloud technologies, social media, mobile communications, and big data!

You may be wondering what all this has to do with seven out of ten cyber incidents occurring due to human error. As a matter of fact, this statistic means everything! As technology has evolved rapidly in all aspects, cyber security tools such as firewalls, anti-malware software, email protection solutions, and a host of other things have also gotten a lot better. This means that it became harder for bad guys and gals to bypass protective security technologies. To counter this, bad actors figured out that it was a lot easier, cheaper, and worthwhile to target humans instead! They understood that instead of trying to spend time and money to hack people's passwords, it was so much easier to trick users into revealing them. Simple, isn't it?

On the topic of bad actors, let's get a better understanding of who these people typically are. I have roughly categorized them into the following groups:

- **The Expert Cyber-Criminal:** These are really smart people who have decided to use their talents for nefarious purposes. They use sophisticated tools and techniques to conduct their activities, with the objective generally being to make money.

- **The Wannabe Hacker:** These people have the intentions of expert cyber-criminals but not the same skill level. They also tend to have fragile egos and just a general bad attitude toward life, which results in them also launching cyber-attacks just to create chaos and maybe feel better about themselves. The widespread and easy availability of automated hacking tools has made it easier for a lot of wannabes to launch cyber-attacks. Anyone with a computer and fifty bucks can buy a malware kit on the dark web, so the access to malicious tools and the ability to learn how to use them have never been this easy. The barrier to entry into the shady world of cybercrime is unfortunately low these days.

- **The Nation:** These are governments or government-backed organizations that indulge in cyber-attacks for a multitude of reasons. These include:

  - taking the shortcut to economic prosperity by stealing intellectual property, research, and trade secrets from other countries.
  - gaining strategic advantage in conflicts by acquiring capabilities to launch destructive cyber-attacks on utilities, transportation systems, and finance machinery. This basically

includes bringing a country to its knees when war-like situations flare up.

o   stealing information to get advantages in matters of diplomacy, trade negotiations, and international resolutions.

• **The Saboteur:** These are disgruntled people in organizations who do bad things to make money or hurt their employer by causing losses and/or embarrassment.

• **The Mafia:** The name says it all. Organized crime gangs who have started using cyber-attacks to further their cause. This generally involves making money. A big reason why the mafia has entered the world of cybercrime is that rates of attribution and prosecution for cybercrime are abysmal compared to the crime in the physical world.

- **The Hacktivist:** These are people who hack or create cyber disruptions for the purpose of making a political or social point.

To understand the allure of cybercrime, let's pick an admittedly over-simplified example to illustrate the point. If some thugs approach someone walking out of a bank with sizeable cash and attempt to rob him, they'll probably be doomed to a terrible fate thanks to all sorts of physical security means, including guards, guns, and gates. Not to mention surveillance cameras everywhere, which will make any escape a short-lived and futile effort. Also, laws on these kinds of issues are very clear. The criminals will be serving time in prison for a lot longer than they'd like.

Now, contrast that with a very common attack in the cyber world called "payroll diversion." This attack uses phishing emails to trick an employee into revealing their account login information. The bad actor then uses this information to redirect payroll from one direct deposit location to another, sending the next salary earnings to an account they have direct or indirect control over. It is much harder to identify the criminal in this case, and it's very likely that they're operating from a different country. This makes it extremely difficult to bring them to justice even if authorities identify them. This is the current reality of cybercrime and why it is so lucrative to all sorts of bad actors. Attribution and prosecution of crime is much harder in the cyber world than it is in the physical world.

Another aspect to consider is how the nature of work has changed. Take a look around in airports, trains, coffee shops, or shopping malls. You'll find people hooked onto their screens, scrolling or typing on them. These smart devices have reshaped how we work! They are called smartphones, but they're more computers than phones. I make this comment because I see people use these devices for everything other than talking.

This change has also meant there is no traditional network perimeter anymore. There are no old-school castles or walls or forts that people can safely sit behind and think they're safe. Work now happens on the move and in homes. Old-school protection controls don't work anymore in this new world. With the walls and perimeters collapsing, humans have become the new firewalls! It is also worth noting that technical security controls typically tend to be much weaker at people's homes and on the move, further increasing the importance of the human factor!

Essentially, humans are far too often all that stand between order and the chaos of stolen information, scams, fraud, and other widespread technology-facilitated disruptions. This is precisely why we need to design and communicate cyber awareness well to ensure that the message is understood, comprehended, and applied. The seven rules described in this book will enable you to achieve these outcomes.

"Nothing in life is to be feared, it is only to be understood. Now is the time to understand more, so that we may fear less."

Marie Curie

4 Rule 1: Stop Relying on Bad News

The experts in the cyber security world have sadly become convicts of their own convictions. They have fallen prey to the psychological phenomenon known as "group think"—where desire for conformity in the group results in irrational outcomes that are unchanged, even in the face of compelling evidence to the contrary. This has led the cyber security community to unwittingly adopt fear, uncertainty, and doubt as their primary vehicles of communication.

Just look at all the latest news about cyber security. It is full of negativity, with announcements of security breaches into millions of personal records occurring almost daily. If it's not the breaches, it's scary news related to invasions of people's privacy and crippling cyber-attacks that have brought companies to their knees. I just saw a news article that talked about two billion personal records recently being leaked! Yes, that's billion with a B! At the time of writing this book, that equates to around a quarter of the entire population of planet Earth.

Now, these incidents are all true and very distressing, and they certainly need to be reported on. My issue is with the asinine nature of intellectual laziness that the cyber security community has engaged in by exclusively using bad news and relying on fear as the awareness mechanism to influence human behaviour. Just look at all the awareness materials around cyber security, filled with images of hoody-wearing hackers, locks and keys, random binary code reminiscent of a movie from the 1990s, and some going as far as to show a ticking bomb to make a point.

Seriously? Is this the best we can do?

Starting every security awareness presentation with some scary news about a multi-million-dollar cyber breach due to phishing hasn't stopped people from clicking on phishing emails! In the best of circumstances, that kind of shock effect may work for a couple of days when the news about the breach is fresh, but the fundamental behaviour of people doesn't change. It just doesn't work that way over the long term! How do we know this? Because if it actually changed human behaviour, we wouldn't see majority of cyber security incidents occurring due to human error and billions of dollars being lost due to email scams! These numbers are getting worse, not better, despite more money being thrown at the problem.

As Albert Einstein so astutely said, "The definition of insanity is to do the same thing over and over expecting a different result." It should be recognized that people largely use technology to solve problems and improve their lives, which are fundamentally positive and hopeful ambitions. When cyber security messaging comes across as full of negativity and fear, it is bound to be viewed, at least at some basic level, as a threat to the same people's hopeful ambitions. Generally speaking, we need to understand this basic human attribute—fear generally induces inaction, while positive reinforcements and rewards encourage the human tendency to seek progress through action.

Since cyber security is fundamentally a human issue, we need to understand how human beings actually learn. So let's look at real psychological data on human learning.

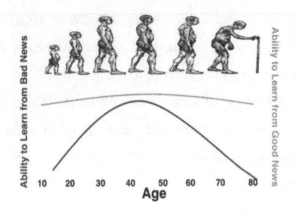

The above image illustrates how humans consistently learn better from good news as opposed to bad news. It is taken from a famous presentation (TEDx Talks 2014) by Dr. Tali Sharot on human learning and behaviour change. Dr. Sharot is a renowned author and professor of cognitive neuroscience at University College London.

The image is based on comprehensive scientific studies (Moutsiana, Garrett, Clarke, Lotto, Blakemore, and Sharot 2013) (Chowdhury, Sharot, Wolfe, Düzel, and Dolan 2014) that show across various age groups, people are more receptive to information they consider favourable than information they don't want to hear. Basically, the ability to learn from good news, such as positive reinforcement and an optimistic future, remained quite stable throughout the life span, but the ability to learn from bad news, such as warnings, deteriorated significantly from age forty onward.

The interesting thing to note is that across all age groups, the ability to learn from good news always stayed higher than the ability to learn from bad news. As you can see from the trends in the image, the gap in learning between good versus bad news is especially large after age sixty. This fact is extremely significant, as you'll soon discover.

Now, the Internet Crime Center publishes regular reports (https://www.ic3.gov) based on the cybercrimes reported to the Federal Bureau of Investigation (FBI). Over the years, one trend in these reports has remained constant—older people, especially those over the age of sixty, are consistently more impacted by cybercrime, such as scams and email-based attacks. Not only does this group have the highest number of victims, but they also lose the largest amount of money. However, we just saw from the aforementioned study on human learning that the older age group was also the least likely to learn from bad news. Basically, this means that in our infinite wisdom, we're using the least effective way to communicate cyber security to the group that needs it the most! And then we wonder why most cyber awareness efforts fail.

Interestingly, we're noticing a shift in awareness campaigns in non-cyber areas such as public anti-smoking campaigns. Anti-smoking campaigns are now reducing their sole reliance on the use of bad news, such as cigarette smoking will kill you. The single-minded focus on negative news has not helped smokers quit. In fact, there's plenty of anecdotal evidence that putting scary pictures on cigarette packets actually causes more stress, which leads to people smoking even more! To address this, the anti-smoking campaigns are now slowly but steadily highlighting the positive things you can achieve or witness in your life if you kick the habit, such as becoming a better athlete or being there to witness the special moments as your children grow up, graduate, get married, and have babies. The campaigns have also adopted a more human touch by acknowledging that it's okay if you stumble in your efforts to quit. You just have to keep moving ahead.

A great alternative approach that works to improve human behaviour is to use social acceptance and a healthy amount of peer-pressure.

A real-life example of this is the British tax agency, Her Majesty's Revenue and Customs (HMRC). In the past, they sent reminder letters to delinquent taxpayers stressing the importance of paying taxes on time. This clearly wasn't helping much. To address this, they applied the approach of using positive peer pressure and social acceptance by adding a single line—"Nine out of ten people in the UK pay their tax on time." That's it. Just this simple addition contributed to increased tax compliance by 15%! (UK Government Cabinet Office 2012) Interestingly, it was observed that the line was more effective at raising compliance rates when followed by the statement—"You are one of the few who have not paid us yet." Furthermore, messages that emphasised localised comparisons resulted in superior outcomes. HMRC noticed that compliance rose 6.8% when taxpayers were told they were one of few delinquents in their hometowns.

These percentages may appear small, but in context of the size of the British economy, these numbers can end up making a difference of billions of dollars of additional revenue!

I've personally experienced the power of starting with positive imagery during presentations on cyber security issues. I was preparing a presentation on practical ways to secure information and applications in cloud environments as part of my talk at a technology forum in Sydney. This topic, as you may imagine, is quite technical and inherently dry. There is a risk of losing the audience's interest due to the nature of the discussion. However, as always, I was determined to make this talk engaging, powerful, and thereby ensure that the advice I was offering was actually being used. To this end, as opposed to the traditional approach of starting presentations with statistics and scary numbers of recent cloud computing breaches, I started with a fascinating image that showed highlights of what happens every minute of every day on the internet. For example, in 2017, every minute of every day, Google conducted nearly 3.7 million searches, YouTube users watched 4.1 million videos, Instagram users posted 46,000 photos, Twitter users sent 456,000 tweets, Amazon made around $259,000 in sales, and Netflix users streamed nearly 70,000 hours of content!

The point of showing this image was to highlight how our lives have fundamentally transformed due to technology, and this wouldn't be possible without the flexibility, scalability, and economics of cloud computing. I have included links to similar images in the resources section of the book. Now, when I started with this image, I emphatically made a positive point about the importance of securing cloud computing environments to ensure our collective progress through technology. Right at the start, I was able to engage my audience, which ensured their active attention and participation for the rest of my presentation.

The success of this talk led to requests for me to present it at multiple industry forums and finally culminated with me presenting on cloud security at the Australian Information Security Association's National Conference in Sydney. This conference is one of the largest and most prestigious cyber gatherings in the country, so while I was thrilled for the opportunity, I also gathered more tangible evidence that positive messaging can indeed work in the cyber security awareness area.

To be clear, I'm not saying that relevant news about cyber breaches or dangers associated with cyber threats should be ignored in awareness messages. Of course, they have an important place in specific awareness efforts. However, my point is that we shouldn't rely exclusively on these topics to affect change.

I encourage you to explore positive options that give people a sense of control and drive them toward action. I urge you to apply creative thinking to cyber security awareness efforts. I know it's hard to break years of bad patterns of exclusively using scary news to communicate cyber security. But we owe it to our audience, our fellow citizens, and the public at large to do our best to bring about a positive change.

Just remember this simple fact—an overwhelming majority of your people want to do the right thing. You need to make it easier for them to understand what that is and how to do it.

Let's look at "Rule 2 – Don't Be Boring" to see guidance and examples of creating good cyber content that doesn't only rely on bad news.

"I can excuse everything but boredom. Boring people don't have to stay that way."

Hedy Lamarr

5   Rule 2: Don't Be Boring

I could write an entire book solely dedicated to this rule, and content creation is a topic that·has tons of books all to itself. However, for the purpose of this book, it is enough to understand that for cyber awareness to be effective, the content must be entertaining and relevant. I consider the current state of atrociously boring content as one of the most egregious failures in the cyber awareness world. The awareness content is usually bland with no humour whose sole purpose appears to be curing insomnia. I equate it to messages as exciting as, "Eat salad and exercise," and we know how well this message is working out with the ever-rising obesity rates globally.

Let's start making good content in the cyber world by creating messages that are meaningful AND have some humour to them. Don't be bashful of being edgy. Throw overtly formal language, jargon, and the lousy hoody-wearing hacker pictures out the window. Create good content so people are actually interested in reading what you have to say. Be authentic. Make your efforts engaging and fun. Use different types of media.

I'll share a simple personal example from my time with a large Australian company that shows the power of good content. The objective of my awareness message was to reduce the number of devices with unpatched or out of date software. This is an important control to protect against hackers looking to break into systems. The awareness message was intended to be posted on the company intranet to get maximum attention from users to update their systems. I used a funny picture of a pirate with an eye patch saying, "Patches are not just for pirates!" The headline was catchy. The message accompanying the picture explained that patches are also important for your devices and included a link to actionable quick tips to apply the latest updates.

Use of the funny but relevant picture got people's attention. In this age of information overload, attention is gold for content promotion. The content stood out amongst a barrage of other boring corporate content for its uniqueness. People engaged with the article by liking, sharing, and commenting, which then resulted in more people reading it. Do you think people would have paid attention if I would have said something like,

"Patch your devices since hackers exploit vulnerabilities in unpatched systems?" Nope. That is bland and boring. It gets negligible attention and, as a result, would be totally ineffective.

I truly believe in the adage that a picture speaks more than a thousand words. I highly recommend you include catchy images as part of your awareness messaging in order to make your lessons more interesting and memorable.

Another example where opening a presentation with a powerful image served me well is when I was presenting on Bitcoin and its underlying technology, called Blockchain. This was at a time before the word "cryptocurrency" went mainstream, with major media attention and several documentaries on the topic. Now, I could have started my presentation with talking about encryption and protocols of this new technology, but that would have been boring. Also, the audience was a mix of people with different levels of management and technical experience. Opening with boring technical content would have risked losing a fair bit of them. Instead, I started my presentation with a graph showing massive fluctuations in prices of Bitcoin in Australian dollars over a short period of time. These prices varied dramatically from a few hundred dollars to thousands of dollars, all in a matter of weeks.

I noticed from the audience's reactions that they were now engaged. They saw Bitcoin as something real. Something that had tangible monetary value. Something that people across the world were starting to use and were willing to pay good "real" money for. Once I had caught their full attention and interest, the rest of the presentation was a success, with complete audience engagement.

Another brilliant example of good content is a hilarious awareness message I saw on the internet that equated the bad practice of using the same passwords on different websites with using the same toothbrush to brush your teeth and scrub the toilet. This succinctly makes people realize how terrible it is to use the same passwords across different websites—a big risk being that if one of these websites is hacked, all your other accounts are also at risk. Imagine the damage possible if one of these accounts is the login to your banking website!

I have seen the same message being communicated through a picture of a cute puppy holding a toothbrush and toothpaste, the premise being that you wouldn't use the same toothbrush to brush your teeth as well as your dog's—so why use the same password across different accounts? This practice essentially communicates an important idea through a combination of humour and disgust. Both these emotions have powerful retention abilities that allow messages to stick in people's minds.

We absolutely need to leverage the power of emotions to get our message across. Famous neuroscientist, Antonio Damasio, through his extensive research and 1994 book, *Descartes' Error: Emotion, Reason, and the Human Brain*, effectively made the case that humans can't make good decisions if their emotions are impaired. In addition to enabling actions and decisions, emotions exhibited by others can also impact our own physical state.

California-based psychologist Wendy Mendes and her team demonstrated through their study (Waters, West, Karnilowicz, and Mendes 2017) that emotions felt by mothers directly influenced their infants' behaviour, even when they were in separate rooms.

This phenomenon, however, isn't just restricted to mothers and infants. We've all felt the rush of adrenaline through our bodies when listening to an inspirational speech or when our favourite athletes are celebrating after a close championship win! The ability to feel pleasure, pain, and stress from others is something we are seemingly born with.

A practical approach to creating powerful content that evokes emotions is to make it personal! You should make it raw and real, and this is where I recommend aligning your content with the message of online safety, or eSafety. Online safety goes beyond traditional cyber discussions, where the focus is on protecting devices and information. Online safety includes considerations for issues such as cyber bullying, revenge porn, and image-based and technology-facilitated abuse. These issues impact people's well-being, including their mental and physical health.

Let's look at an example of leveraging the connection between cyber security and physical safety as part of security messaging. Now, we all want to raise awareness in our organizations about the significance of privacy legislations and ensuring the security of our customers' personal information. While privacy is certainly important, it's not very interesting to talk about. The challenge is making it interesting so that people are more diligent in ensuring the protection of the sensitive information under their care. This is a scenario where making things truly personal can help. The awareness messaging can articulate that when customer records are breached due to lack of diligence on our part, we are impacting the lives of real people who trusted us with their personal information. While a breach will most likely be a violation of privacy regulations, the problems can be seriously compounded in situations where a customer has fled a domestic violence situation and, as a result of the data breach, their new address or related information is out in the public domain. This can put them at high risk of physical harm if the information falls into the hands of an abusive ex-partner. This message now truly resonates at a personal level and highlights the close relationship between cyber security and physical safety.

We can use this approach to make issues tangible for our people as opposed to getting bogged down by focusing merely on data breach or privacy legislations.

The interesting thing is that good practices recommended for online safety have significant overlaps with those for cyber security. The idea is if you help protect people in their own homes, it will also lead to a heightened awareness in the workplace. Furthermore, harness the power of story-telling and analogies to make this connection. Consider the following examples:

If you are trying to educate users on protecting themselves by not revealing sensitive information through phishing emails or to scamsters using phone calls and texts, you can draw an analogy by asking them if they would divulge sensitive information such as their social security number, tax file number, or bank details to a stranger on a train without adequately challenging their purpose and the need for them to know the information. No, of course they wouldn't. Then why wouldn't they employ similar vigilance when it comes to activities online or over the phone? This will get your users' attention because it's the same impact, just a different medium of the bad event happening. This is a much more engaging way of starting awareness conversations and transferring personal safety to work security.

Let's look at another example.

We like to educate users to not write their passwords and leave them unprotected in open spaces. Instead, we'd like them to use password managers such as LastPass or KeePass to securely manage their different passwords. To get this message across, let's question your audience if they would ever leave their valuable jewellery unprotected in an open area. Of course they wouldn't! They'd lock it and tuck it away safely while protecting the keys or codes to the safe with all possible vigilance. Why would they not apply the same care to protecting their passwords? If someone nefarious gets a hold of their password, they can use it to log into their accounts and access very sensitive information about them, their family, their kids, and their customers.

This is because our lives are now online—we bank online, and so much of our private moments such as messages and pictures live in our email inboxes, social media websites, and online storage, such as Google Drive and OneDrive. All this information is at risk when our passwords are compromised. This problem is exacerbated by the fact that most people just reuse the same password for all their accounts.

Another message that fits well with the analogy of not leaving valuables unattended is not leaving devices such as laptops and smartphones unattended in public places. This is because the information on these devices is nearly as valuable as physical valuables. After all, information is the currency of our modern digital age.

Using examples like these will immediately connect with your audience and further your chances of making a difference in their behaviour.

A tricky but common challenge in cyber awareness is overcoming apathy and inaction among users who think they have nothing valuable that a hacker might want or feel they have nothing to hide. To address this, simply ask your audience if they'd share their unlocked smartphone at this exact moment with a stranger who is allowed to install any app on it. You'd start noticing a fair bit of reluctance, for good reason. By handing over their unlocked phones, they're exposing themselves to the possibility of someone going through all sorts of personal messages, correspondence, and images on there. Also, if the person decides to install malicious applications on your phone, they can control the device, listen to your conversations, and track your movements. This has the potential to cause a lot of damage, including physical harm. This scenario is unfortunately playing out all too often these days, with insecure partners or abusive exes using sextortion or technology-based monitoring to cause immense distress to the victims. Using powerful personal stories like these will ensure your security awareness content gets the attention it deserves.

While on the topic of online safety, at the time of writing this book, Australia is the only country in the world that has a government appointed commissioner specifically dedicated to eSafety. I have personally worked with this office and commend them for the great service they provide. I have included links to valuable resources from the commissioner's office in the resources section of this book. I am optimistic that more countries will follow suit by providing dedicated resources toward online safety.

One more example of the power of analogies. We educate users on the risks of tailgating, which is when people physically follow you closely to get unauthorized entry into offices, or do things like pretend they have forgotten their entry pass or have their hands full with coffee in order to ask you to let them in. This opens up a lot of risks, including theft of expensive computing devices containing valuable data and sensitive paper records as well as the risk of physical harm. Despite continuous awareness on this issue, the problem of tailgating still stubbornly persists. To address this, ask your audience if they would allow a stranger, no matter how nice they seem, to just enter their homes without first asking them their business and some sort of identification so they can prove they are who they say they are. Why should the same care not be applied at workplaces or offices? The point again is you need to make the message real to people for it to grab their attention. I also strongly recommend that you keep your awareness messages simple and follow the advice of Mark Twain—avoid using a five-dollar word when a fifty-cent word will suffice.

If you want more ideas for analogies to improve your awareness programs, have a look at *The Analogies*

Project (https://theanalogiesproject.org/) for some excellent resources.

Another approach to creating engagement and interest in your security awareness program is through rewarding your users and providing them recognition through the use of competitions. We humans are social animals and love to feel valued and appreciated by our peers. Getting the most out of this basic human tendency is a positive step toward influencing behaviour.

Let's look at a practical example. During my time with a large Australian organization, I organized a phishing email writing competition to create awareness about the important issue of phishing and scams. Essentially, the competitors had to write a good phishing email designed to trick the victim into disclosing some sensitive information. To safeguard against unintended consequences, I made sure that users understood what they could or couldn't do—an obvious no-no being they couldn't phish anyone for real. To ensure a controlled outcome, I asked them to submit their phishing email entry on a word document with no embedded links or macros. The intent was to get them thinking creatively as hackers and social engineers and not allow the technically skilled to have an unfair advantage. This helped level the playing field and encouraged creativity from all different groups. As an incentive, a modest but meaningful prize was offered to the winner.

I'm delighted to say that the response to the competition was amazing. We got all kinds of great entries, ranging from the extremely ingenious to the delightfully hilarious. The winning entry was judged by a member of the organization's senior leadership, and the winner received a great personal congratulations along with a nice gift from the senior leader. While only one person actually won the competition, in reality, the whole organization was the winner. The competition created great awareness around the topic of phishing and provided much needed visibility to all the tools and resources available to the employees through the security awareness website. The winning entry also became a part of the overall awareness messaging content, which was an added bonus!

This is just one of the ways in which competition can turn potentially dry topics into something exciting.

Another idea for a competition is designing a cyber mascot! The winning mascot would be proudly displayed on all future security awareness messages and materials. While this will drive excitement and engagement around cyber security, there is also the added benefit of getting recognizable branding for the awareness materials. Mascots are powerful, and if done correctly, they can make a message truly stand out. The use of Smokey Bear by the US Forest Service to raise awareness about wildfires is a classic example of this. Smokey now even has his own Twitter account!

When the mascot is developed through a friendly competition and by one of your own, there will be a sense of ownership to it from the rest of the organization and, of course, awesome brand recognition!

A useful tip if you are running competitions: Always remember to make people feel special and rewarded for their participation. Rewarding good behaviour is essential for showing the organization's appreciation for people who demonstrate commitment toward protecting its most valuable assets.

The prizes or rewards don't have to be big in monetary value to be meaningful. I have used things like free movie tickets and coffee gift cards as prizes for winners of competitions. A small ceremony with some juice and donuts and the presence of a senior executive to hand the prize to the winner goes a long way. This makes the winners feel special and also attracts more people to attend the ceremony, which has the added benefit of kindling their desire to win the next cyber competition. From personal observation, never underestimate the power of free food to attract a crowd. Of course, if you can manage to get a sizeable financial award, more power to you!

As a way of creating an ongoing focus on rewarding good cyber behaviour, you can propose creating friendly competition between departments to see which has the most employees exhibiting good security behaviours. The winning criteria can be based on the percentage of employees who participate in security awareness activities, engage with security content posted on internal forums, or serve as valuable advocates of cyber security. You can schedule this competition over the course of six months with monthly statistics published on how each participating department is doing. At the end of the competition, the winning department can be presented a trophy, ideally by the CEO—but if that's too difficult, then by the CIO or CISO. You can also present an individual award to the employee who performed the best during this six-month cycle regardless of the department they belong to.

The options of making things exciting and rewarding good behaviours are only limited by your imagination!

If you had to take away only one thing from this book, I suggest you incorporate this rule in your awareness efforts. Make it interesting. Make it relevant. Make it real. Our diminishing attention spans desperately need it.

"Goals transform a random walk into a chase."

Mihaly Csikszentmihalyi

6   Rule 3: Be SMART in Your Approach

It seems fairly obvious that we need defined objectives to be successful in our endeavours. However, there's plenty of evidence in our daily lives that we don't always necessarily abide by this rule. For example, let's consider the oh-so-common case of going to a department store without a list of specific items to buy. We have all been there. With no list, more often than not, we end up buying things we just didn't need. We spend money we didn't plan on spending and probably forget to buy things we set out to purchase in the first place!

This happens all the time—but why? I propose that it's because of a simple concept we all intuitively understand but somehow fail to practice. Unless we have defined what we are trying to achieve, we will not achieve it successfully or will achieve it at much greater cost and effort than planned. I see this exact scenario plague cyber security awareness efforts all the time!

The vast majority of security awareness programs are run in an ad hoc manner without defined objectives. Half-baked objectives are then hurriedly bolted on retrospectively when questions are asked about the value of investment and program effectiveness.

Do you want to know if your awareness efforts or program will be successful? Go ahead and answer these questions.

- What exactly is your security awareness program intending to achieve and how do you measure its progress?
- What happens if the awareness program doesn't achieve its objective? Can you quantify the adverse outcome?

If you can't answer these questions with certainty and clarity, I hate to break it to you, but your awareness program will fail. You don't have clearly defined objectives and metrics and thus are lacking a foundational element of success.

Not to worry, though. By utilizing the information provided in this chapter, you'll be able to define clear objectives and metrics and build yourself a strong base for success.

Let's get started. Cyber security awareness objectives usually fall under the following two categories.

1. To inform, so your audience has baseline knowledge of cyber threats and understands the steps to protect themselves.
2. To influence decision-making and motivate secure behaviours in your audience to reduce the likelihood of the most significant cyber risks.

The objectives in category one typically relate to ensuring your audience understands general cyber security issues and is made aware of their responsibilities when working with organizational information and systems. I consider this category of objectives to be the very basic level of maturity. This is also typically where I see most cyber awareness programs who claim to have defined objectives operate. Progress toward these objectives are measured through tracking (a) the number of users who have completed general cyber awareness training and (b) user acknowledgement that they have read and understood organizational policy requirements. It is generally expected that both these numbers should be close to 100%.

I don't think there is anything terribly wrong with these objectives, and they're better than having no objectives at all since they do inform users on cyber security issues, are necessary to meet compliance obligations, and provide organizations with the ability to discipline employees when they engage in undesirable or unlawful behaviour. However, I strongly believe that the mere act of informing and getting acknowledgement does very little to move the needle toward good security practices. The true focus of cyber security awareness needs to be on comprehension and application of the information. The value of knowledge, after all, lies in its application. Therefore, I suggest channelling more of your program and awareness efforts into the second category, which is to motivate positive changes in user behaviour.

To get a better sense of how good awareness objectives operate in the non-cyber realm, consider the case of cigarette smoking. It is fair to say that governments all over the world have recognized cigarette smoking as one of the most serious risks to public health and wellness. In response, governments have launched aggressive public anti-smoking campaigns intended to influence decision-making and change the behaviours of current and potential smokers. The objective of this campaign is very clear—to get current smokers to quit and discourage potential smokers in order to improve overall public health and wellness.

This clarity of objective allows the definition of good metrics to measure the effectiveness of the campaign. We can track if there is a decline in the number of current smokers due to them quitting and the overall reduction in the average number of new smokers. If both these numbers continue to trend downward, we can call the awareness campaign effective. If, however, these numbers keep rising, then there's clearly a need to make changes to the awareness campaign and the overall public policy. In either case, we are able to measure the success or failure of awareness efforts with a fair degree of objectivity. We need to design our cyber security awareness programs in the same way. They need to be focused on changing specific behaviours that matter the most to us based on the nature of our business.

In summary, your objectives need to clearly define the issue you're trying to address, which will help identify the specific behaviours you need to influence.

The first step in this process is to clearly understand the primary business functions of your organization. This will enable identification of the cyber security risks that are of most significance to the organization. I put emphasis on the word "most" since you want to focus your efforts on issues that give you the most value for your investments. As a rule of thumb, good security awareness programs are typically focused on addressing three or four key cyber risks.

Let's look at an example of how the entire process of key cyber risk identification leads to the definition of objectives, which then distinguishes the behaviours that the awareness programs need to influence.

Consider a scenario where your organization is a healthcare centre in the business of treating patients and improving their quality of life. In the course of your business, you will end up with a lot of sensitive personal information about your patients and their families. One of the key cyber risks in this scenario is that sensitive information trusted to you by your patients is stolen or publicly disclosed. This would be devastating for your patients and potentially subject them to emotional trauma at a time when they are already vulnerable.

Let's identify another cyber risk relevant to this scenario. To treat your patients efficiently, you likely have an electronic patient management system that holds patient records (e.g., allergies to medications, previous surgical history, X-rays, etc.). Consider what would happen if you couldn't access this system, or worse, lost the records completely due to a virus or malware attack. A common malware attack in this scenario could be a ransomware attack, which would lock all your files until you pay ransom to the bad actor to unlock your system. Unfortunately, the chances of you getting your files back even after paying the ransom are slim to none.

Now, both the aforementioned cyber risks really matter to you. They would matter to you more than a cyber risk scenario where your center's public website containing general information about your practice is unavailable for a few days. Your business or patients aren't heavily impacted by this since the website is for informational purposes and not to directly generate revenue or treat patients.

However, the scenario of the website being unavailable would rank much higher on the key risk scale if you were an e-commerce company like eBay and relied on your website as the predominant means to generate revenue. The amount of losses in this case would be astronomical!

We can see how every business has a different cyber risk profile, and you need to know yours. The topic of cyber risk management is beyond the scope of this book and has several books and entire bodies of knowledge dedicated to it. If you're interested in learning more about the subject, I have provided some useful links in the resources chapter.

Now, continuing with our healthcare center scenario. Since we have identified the two main cyber risks, you can now design a cyber security awareness program focused on influencing behaviours that are most relevant to these issues. See, we're getting specific now! This is exactly where we want to be.

Specific behaviour changes in this case may include:

- Training staff and users to recognize suspicious emails, report them, and under no circumstances open attachments or click on links within them.

Now let's make a direct link between this behaviour and the two cyber risks:

- Falling for phishing emails could result in disclosure of usernames and passwords, thus leading to your users' accounts being hacked. Now the bad actor can use these details to access, steal, and disclose sensitive patient information.
- Clicking on suspicious links or opening attachments in malicious emails may result in malware getting installed on your systems, which causes them to become unstable and

unavailable. Some sophisticated malware can now move from one system to another very quickly and can make all the systems in your clinic unavailable. This scary scenario unfolded during the global WannaCry ransomware attack and caused the loss of billions of dollars worldwide, severely impacting many hospitals' abilities to treat patients. You can find more information on this attack by searching for the term "WannaCry" on your favourite search engine.

Now that you have identified the behaviours you want to influence, you can clearly define objectives for your security awareness program and include measurements to track their progress.

One of the key metrics to measure success in this example is to see a reduction in the amount of phishing emails that people respond to or click on, also called "click-rate." Another good metric would be tracking the number of incidents that occurred due to email-based attacks.

What gets measured gets managed. What gets managed delivers value. Your cyber security awareness program is now starting to show value!

The above example is admittedly simplistic but can easily be extrapolated for any security awareness program if the process of understanding the business and identifying key cyber risks is followed.

Over the course of my career, I have worked with and observed several large organizations that have thousands of employees, a global footprint, many different business areas, and millions of sensitive personal records. Even for organizations of this scale and complexity, the approach I have outlined has worked very well.

Considering the crucial nature of objectives and measurements to the success of your security awareness program, let's do a bit of a deep-dive through some more examples.

A good objective should have SMART attributes. By SMART, I mean it should be Specific, Measurable, Actionable, Relevant, and Time-bound. The SMART acronym has been around since the 1980s and is widely used across different industries for defining good objectives and goals. An example of a SMART objective in the cyber awareness context is: After three months of awareness messaging on how to identify suspicious emails, the click-rate on malicious emails should be less than 10% across the organization.

This objective is Specific (focused on suspicious email identification), Measurable (10%), Actionable (you are able to gather this information), Relevant (directly tied to key cyber risk), and Time-bound (specifies the timeframe for the objective—three months).

Phishing simulation campaigns are a great way to measure the progress of your efforts. Here, you basically send a fake phishing email to your target audience and track their response. The tracking includes how many recipients clicked on the phishing links within the email—also known as click-rate—how many users reported the email to your helpdesk or the security team, what departments had more users falling for the phishing email, and whether or not there was a difference in click-rate between users who opened the email on their phones versus laptops and desktops. All these attributes give you excellent insight into the effectiveness of your awareness efforts and provide you with actionable intelligence on the problem areas.

Depending on the tool you use to run the campaign, you can craft emails with varying levels of sophistication and scenarios. You can make them very realistic by using internal "from" email addresses or emails coming from a domain very similar to your own company's.

There are several good products that provide this capability, such as Proofpoint Wombat technologies and Cofense PhishMe. There are some open source tools as well, but they require advanced technical expertise for their customization. I have provided links to these products and tools in the resources section. However, considering the pace at which these tools evolve, I recommend you go to my website, for the latest links and updates: https://www.chiragdjoshi.com/

A quick word of advice on phishing simulation campaigns—any phishing simulation campaign should be conducted in consultation with and support of your senior management and IT teams. To get the most value from this exercise, provide your users with a friendly message if they click on the fake phishing link. The message should inform them that this was an internal testing exercise intended to improve their awareness to real-world cyber risks. You should assure them that their passwords haven't been compromised or recorded. You should also use this opportunity to provide a learning moment where you point out what they missed and include a link to more information on how they can protect themselves in the future. Some organizations conduct these campaigns monthly and require users who have repeatedly fallen for phishing emails to undergo formal retraining. I suggest you take an empathetic approach to educating users who fall for phishing emails. In my experience, a punishment-based approach doesn't work too well for long term behaviour change. I recommend you start slow with these exercises and then adapt as required. Let's learn to crawl first before we start walking.

Let's look at another example of a SMART objective. Within two month of awareness activities around password security, less than 5% of employees will have passwords written and left unsecured in open areas.

In order to track progress of your efforts, you can conduct or organize physical security walkthroughs in your offices after hours to detect instances of written passwords posted on monitors or left in open areas.

You can use the SMART objective approach for measuring effectiveness of any awareness or training initiatives on behaviour change. It's almost like magic!

Another great source of inspiration for designing good objectives can come from within the cyber security area itself. Far too often, what we seek is right in front of us. Let's consider cyber security technologies like anti-malware and antivirus products.

The objective for these tools is well-defined: to stop or prevent malicious software from installing or running on your devices. Since the objective is clear, it is easy to measure if the control is successful or not based on the number of devices that have the tool installed but are still infected with malware.

Security awareness also needs to be treated as a key control, with clearly defined objectives and measurements for success. The time has come to stop running security awareness programs on intuition, the latest news story, and other ad hoc practices. It simply does not work.

A practical way to identify and gain agreement on objectives and measurements in your organization is through structured one-on-one conversations and workshops or focus group sessions with subject matter experts from different areas of your organization. These could include people from human resources, finance, legal, IT, and business specific areas such as sales, marketing, production, customer support, and facilities management.

Depending on the size of the organization, and to accommodate people's availability, you'll most likely end up organizing several focus group sessions. These focus groups should cover a representative sample of your main lines of business and support functions.

To get the most value from these sessions and conversations, you need to have a list of clear objectives and a charismatic facilitator who can manage the group to ensure that all voices are heard and that some strong personalities aren't hijacking the conversation.

The main outcomes you want from the conversations and focus groups are:

1. Identify key cyber risks based on business processes.

2. Based on the cyber risks, define objectives and behaviours. Ensure that the objectives are limited to a reasonable number. Remember, if everything is important, then nothing is truly important.

3. Understand the priority of the objectives, which will enable you to plan your awareness messaging and activities.

4. Get agreement on metrics that will be used to track the progress of the awareness program.

5. Identify the best communication channels for different security awareness messages by exploring what is and isn't currently working.

Considering the importance of the identification of cyber risks to the outcome, it is imperative that you have the support and inputs of security and risk management leaders in your organization. You can do this by engaging early and often with them to gain agreement on the desired outcomes.

In summary, I'll emphasize that to achieve your goals, you need to define your objectives clearly. Also, some practical advice—don't start with something that you can't manage. Start with what you can manage, then build upon that.

"It is not our differences that divide us. It is our inability to recognize, accept, and celebrate those differences."

Audre Lorde

7   Rule 4: One Size Barely Fits Anyone

"One size barely fits anyone" is a phrase I like to use when it comes to most security awareness efforts that fail because they rarely account for differences in people, their roles, and the way they work and learn. Think about it—not everybody is receptive to the same kind of messaging. "Different strokes for different folks" is the mantra here. You need to understand how to harness the power of stakeholder analysis or creation of audience profiles to make your cyber security awareness program better.

To perform a useful stakeholder analysis, it is important to understand the demographics and user groups in your organization.

Thanks to the amazing advances in cloud collaboration and productivity applications, video-conferencing, and remote presenting tools, the nature of work has fundamentally changed. We now have far more remote workers who work from homes or different parts of the world. A subsection of this group includes those who are commonly referred to as "road warriors," since their jobs need them to travel extensively and perform most of their tasks through smartphones, iPads, or other mobile devices.

Since a lot of the work performed by remote workers and road warriors happens outside of the traditional physical and network security protections, they are exposed to different cyber risks than people who work inside the confines of a more controlled office environment and central IT networks. This is analogous to the physical security precautions and care you'd take when you're out and about as opposed to the safety and security of your own home. This group needs additional training on how to keep information secure when working remotely. Topics such as physical device security, encryption of data, use of VPN, free public Wi-Fi risks, and regular updates of device software become more relevant.

There are additional considerations for travellers to certain "high risk" countries that have different immigration and security laws. These travellers could be anyone from sales people, executives, researchers, or technical specialists. You need to make them aware of specific travel advice provided by the government, including creating awareness of risks such as the possibility that border officers can ask them to unlock their mobile devices or even confiscate them. There are also some additional risks associated with aggressive internet monitoring that can pose a danger to the confidentiality of information. This unique threat profile requires more specific training on device and information security, as well as a thorough explanation of the role of backups and traveling with clean burner devices; these devices can be wiped on return to ensure no malware is introduced into the company's network.

Another factor is the type of industry you are working in. Ideally, as part of your focus groups conducted based on "Rule 3 – Be SMART in Your Approach," you should have acquired a reasonable sense of business processes in your organization. For example, if you operate in a sector that has a lot of operational technology or industrial control systems environments, such as power generation, transport system controls, or heavy manufacturing, you'll have an engineering team and technicians who are generally out in the field away from the corporate central offices. This group has a different risk profile since a lot of risks to operational technology systems are factors such as malicious USB devices plugged into systems or the risk of physical tailgating into facilities. Also, from my experience, this group tends to have a specific personality type and aren't always very receptive to corporate training mechanisms, which they feel do not reflect their day-to-day lives and are created by office workers who have little knowledge of the reality of the industrial environments.

It is very important to craft an approach for this group that includes real examples of things they deal with. Don't assume they use cloud services or social media as much as a typical office worker. Don't assume they carry a smart device with them all the time. This group responds better to in-person presentations at their location of work when the topic is pertinent to them. Account for these differences, and you'll have a better chance of success.

Special consideration should also be given to the differences between how digital natives learn compared to technology adopters. I view digital natives as people who grew up using and learning all the modern technologies. They tend to be younger in age and learn very differently than folks who didn't grow up with a lot of modern technology; this second group is most likely older in age but has now adopted technology into their work and personal lives. In my experience, the digital natives are more likely to ignore long-winded awareness messages or traditional media emails and respond better to unstructured Just in Time training, which leverages the power of images and short videos. Technology adopters are more likely to respond better to structured awareness training, such as online courses or in-person training.

To make getting started easier for you, here are some standard user groups you're most likely to see in your organizations.

- **Senior Executives:** They are senior-most organizational leaders, typically the C-suite. Due to their significant influence, these groups are often the target of business email scams. This is when a bad actor impersonates them to get other employees to disclose sensitive information or transfer money to the attacker's bank accounts. After all, very few people are able to question an email that directly comes from a CEO! Furthermore, according to the well-respected 2019 *Verizon Data Breach Investigations Report* (Verizon 2019), C-level executives were twelve times more likely to be the target of social engineering related incidents than in years past.

- **Executive Assistants:** They are generally gatekeepers to senior executives and typically have delegated access to their emails, documents, and sensitive files. As such, they are naturally targeted by bad actors to get to the senior leadership's accounts and information.

- **Finance:** These are people with accounts payable and accounts receivable responsibilities. These groups are frequently targeted by bad actors with scam emails and phone calls intended to get money transferred to their bank accounts through fake purchase orders and invoices or through changing payment details on existing vendor files. It's worth noting that large global companies such as Google and Facebook lost millions of dollars through these types of attacks (Fazzini 2019).

- **People who regularly handle sensitive information as part of their jobs:** This includes legal, HR, and frontline customer service agents who directly talk to customers. This group is frequently targeted by bad actors through phishing emails into divulging their login information.

- **Line Managers:** This category refers to the mid-level managers who manage teams and exercise influence over their direct and indirect reports. These people can play an important role in cascading cyber security awareness messages but are also at risk of being targeted by bad actors through phishing or other social engineering attacks.

- **IT teams, including system administrators, developers, and related roles that need privileged access to information systems:** Privileged access can be thought of as administrator level accounts on your device that allow you to install any software or run any application. This group has comparatively more knowledge of cyber issues due to their IT background. However, they should be made aware of scenarios where they are specifically targeted through phishing or other social engineering tactics to obtain their login details, which can provide privileged access to the bad actors. This group also tends to use shared system passwords and should be provided training on password managers and secure password practices. Developers should be provided specific training on creating secure applications from the very beginning through safe coding practices.

- **All users:** This group should be focused on separately, since there are some general security awareness topics that all employees in an organization should know about. This contributes to building baseline knowledge and makes people aware of their responsibilities associated with handling information. General cyber best practices to share with all users include the following topics:

  - Password security best practices that include creating strong passwords, not reusing or sharing passwords, using password managers, and protecting them as you'd protect keys to your safe with valuables.

- Keeping device software up to date.

- Use of anti-malware software, including awareness on ransomware, which is a growing problem. Ransomware is a special type of malware that locks out access to your information by encrypting it, and the only way to unlock it is by paying ransom to the attacker to give you a decryption key. Unfortunately, in most cases, ransomware victims do not get their data back despite paying the ransom.

- Regularly backed up data to the cloud or external media. This is very important to ensure recovery from a device failure or ransomware-type malware attacks.

- Information on social engineering attacks, which are focused on tricking humans as opposed to hacking systems through purely technological means. This should include general information on different types of scams, such as romance scams, remote access scams, and investment scams aimed at obtaining sensitive information and stealing identities and money. The Australian government's website, https://www.scamwatch.gov.au, provides a lot of good resources on this topic. However, I'll provide some information about romance and remote access scams here since they're rising quite rapidly and need attention.

  o Romance scams often take place through online dating websites, but bad actors may also use social media or email to make contact. These bad actors express strong emotions in a relatively short period of time. Once they have gained your trust, they will ask for money, gifts, or banking/credit card details. They may also ask victims to send pictures or videos of themselves, possibly of an intimate nature.

o Remote access scams are where bad actors will contact and try to scare you with false claims—like your computer is infected—and attempt to obtain access to your accounts or devices, in the guise of trying to help you troubleshoot the problem. They'll generally try to sell you a fake security product as well as steal all the valuable information on your devices when given access.

- Cyber security tips when working remotely.

- Securing mobile devices.

- How to spot phishing emails and fake websites.

- How to report suspicious events and cyber incidents.

- Organization policy expectations and requirements for users of company information or equipment.

I have a curated a list of some great free security awareness materials in the resources section that'll ensure you don't need to start from scratch.

Another critical aspect of effective security awareness is reaching the right people through the right communication channels. We've already talked about the importance of communicating differently based on demographics or the level of familiarity with modern technology. Let's look at some of the communication channels you can use to spread the message. These include:

- In-person presentations.
- Short awareness videos.

- Live-streaming cyber awareness sessions or content.
- Digital media, including websites, internal and external social networking applications, intranet, and login pages.
- Emails and electronic newsletters.
- Physical posters that can be posted around the office.
- Digital information boards.
- Quick cyber tips shared at team meetings and other departmental or organization-wide forums.
- Online training videos.
- Desktop wallpapers on company-managed computers.
- Competitions and interactive cyber learning. This can be both in-person or through the use of mobile apps or tools such as surveys and feedback forms.

Of course, only you can decide what channels are available and most effective for your organization and audience. I recommend using the focus groups and workshops described in "Rule 3 – Be SMART in Your Approach" to help you make this decision.

In my experience, in-person training is best suited when doing awareness sessions for senior leaders. Generally, there are a lot of demands on their time, so you need to get to the point quickly and provide clear takeaways. If you're able to score time for an awareness session with multiple senior leaders at the same time, firstly, congratulations! That's no mean feat. You can utilize interactive learning in this session through scenario-based tabletop exercises, where you can simulate or do a walkthrough of a cyber event, such as targeted phishing materializing, and the best course of action to take among available options. The added benefit of scenario-based exercises with senior leaders is that you can have them practice before a real incident so they're well prepared in case something bad actually happens.

As a rule of thumb, in-person sessions are most resource intensive in terms of people's time, logistical arrangements, and cost. They should be used sparingly and with a clear goal in mind. Remember the guidance from "Rule 2 – Don't Be Boring" on the best ways to deliver good content.

To summarise, the success of your awareness program relies heavily on your ability to get your messages understood and applied. Customising messages for your audience will enable its efficacy. So select the best tool for the job and stay away from using a one-size-fits-all approach. Because, as we now know, one size barely fits anyone.

"There are no words to express the abyss between isolation and having one ally. It may be conceded to the mathematician that four is twice two. But two is not twice one; two is two thousand times one."

G. K. Chesterton

8 Rule 5: Harness the Power of Allies

I like the quote from the very popular show *Game of Thrones*—"When the snow falls, and the white winds blow, the lone wolf dies, but the pack survives."

Creating security awareness requires persistence and consistency, as will be described in "Rule 6 – Be Persistent and Consistent." However, the good news is that you don't need to do it all by yourself. And you shouldn't. Actually, let me make it easier—you just can't. Not well, anyway. You need to have allies both within and outside of your organization. Allies can help you sharpen your message, expand your reach, improve your content, increase your knowledge, and most importantly, help you influence behaviour.

Let's look at the groups you can ally with inside your organization:

- **Communications, public relations, and marketing teams:** You absolutely have to develop good relationships and ally with these teams. I'll go ahead and say you need to make them your best friends. These teams can play a very important role in helping you identify the best communication channel for your awareness messages. By the virtue of their professional expertise, they can help you sharpen your content in order to create the most impact.

• **Line managers and influential contacts from business areas:** These groups can be a key enabler for you to cascade your message across different areas. These people can essentially serve as cyber security champions or ambassadors for their business areas. Additionally, most of these people run regular meetings with their direct reports and possibly a monthly meeting with all their direct and indirect reports. By building good relationships, you can put yourself on the agenda for these meetings. This gives you invaluable face-time to communicate your message and solicit real-time feedback. These groups typically have identified responsibilities to ensure their teams are following policies related to IT, so they'll welcome the assistance you are providing with helpful training for their people. This makes it a win-win situation!

- **Legal, privacy, compliance, and risk management teams:** I call these teams the "Assurance Crew." These teams are essentially birds of a feather since they all have a major stake in the protection of sensitive information such as intellectual property, customer or client information, privileged legal communications, and so forth. They also have a keen interest in ensuring the integrity of IT systems, so the digital evidence is admissible in cases of litigations and financial statements are accurate. These groups typically do their own version of awareness sessions to inform people of their responsibilities. By developing strong relationships, you can include your content in their presentation and information materials. You can also potentially get a few minutes in their awareness sessions to talk about cyber security!

- **Physical security teams:** As I mentioned earlier in the book, the worlds of physical security and cyber security have now converged, with both relying heavily on each other. For example, if physical security is inadequate or bypassed, a bad actor can walk into offices and steal devices with sensitive information or tamper with IT infrastructure to create business disruption.

Conversely, an increasing amount of physical security controls such as gates, doors, and cameras are relying on interconnected technology for their operation, monitoring, and surveillance. A successful cyber-attack has the potential to deactivate these controls and essentially cause a large-scale operational disruption or safety event. Working together with physical security teams will enable you to communicate your content to locations outside of corporate offices, in addition to the obvious multiplier effect of your content finding a place in their presentations and information packs.

Now let's look externally. The mantra for success in getting the most out of the power of allies is to network, network, then network again.

- **Professional associations and industry events:** There are some fantastic professional associations that I recommend you become members of. They are ISACA (https://www.isaca.org) and ISC2 (https://www.isc2.org). If you're in Australia, I highly recommend joining the Australian Information Security Association (https://www.aisa.org.au). These international associations have local chapters in many cities across the world, so the probability of you finding one close to you is very high. I am personally a member of all of them and find immense value from them.

  Through your membership and attendance at regular chapter meetings, you will meet many people from your own field as well as people in different industries who have unique life stories and career paths. People in these associations often put competition aside and work together. There is much to learn from discussing challenges, best practices, and sharing experiences with others that can lead to actionable outcomes. The chapter meetings usually have presentations on various topics, ranging from cyber security and risk management to leadership and business communications. Your membership also allows you to access great resources available on their websites. These include white papers, presentations, articles, research on emerging technologies, and various case studies. These resources are powerful tools for your awareness program content and improvements.

These associations also organize many local, national, and international conferences every year, which are fantastic opportunities to learn, connect, and grow!

In addition to these associations, there are other groups such as Cloud Security Alliance (https://www.cloudsecurityalliance.org) and OWASP (https://www.owasp.org), which are usually focused on more detailed technical topics.

- **Government departments and agencies:** Presently, there is so much great cyber awareness content made available by governments that I honestly believe you can build entire awareness programs just using the information they provide.

Also, government agencies are obviously interested in spreading the word on securing the cyber space of their countries, protecting their citizens against scams, and promoting internet safety. In my experience, these departments are very open to working with you on the promotion of awareness activities.

I highly recommend checking https://www.esafety.gov.au/, https://www.scamwatch.gov.au/, and https://www.staysmartonline.gov.au/ for some excellent resources on cyber security and online safety.

- **Meetups and local knowledge-sharing groups:** Not all networking needs to happen through professional associations or conferences. You can search for communication and cyber awareness get-togethers in your area through https://www.meetup.com. I have made a lot of good friends and professional contacts through attending meetups. Most meetups are free, with some charging very low entry fees.

In addition to meetups, you can try to find local knowledge-sharing groups that may be specific to your industry vertical or focused on cyber awareness. In Australia, the Security Influence and Trust (https://www.sitempowers.com) is one of these groups. I encourage you to utilize the power of Google or Bing to find such groups in your local area. If you can't find any, start one or create a meetup group and host an event! If you build it, they will come.

Now that we have discussed some formidable internal and external allies, let's look at other avenues that can help serve as a vehicle for your awareness mission.

- **Leveraging global event days and other opportunistic windows:** Every year in the month of February, Safer Internet Day is observed globally. On this day, governments and organizations all over the world share messages to promote safe and secure online practices. These days are a goldmine for awesome free content that you can use as part of your awareness programs. You should also incorporate these days formally into your awareness activities calendar.

Similarly, there is the Privacy Awareness Week, which in Australia is during the month of May, and the Safe Work Month, which is observed in Australia in October. During these events, privacy and physical security teams do a lot of awareness activities. This is the perfect opportunity for you to include your content and spread the cyber message as part of the overall information.

- You should also keep an eye out for any significant communication activities or events being organized in your company by other teams that would potentially have a sizeable audience. If you have built good relationships, it'll be possible for you to add your awareness messages on the agenda!

In summation, I attribute my success and that of others who I admire in creating cyber security awareness to one common factor—cultivating relationships and forming a powerful network of allies. These allies have helped me achieve meaningful success on mostly very limited budgets. As a bonus, most of these allies have also become lifelong friends and professional connections. So, go ahead and harness the power of allies; I know you can do it, too!

"A little more persistence, a little more effort, and what seemed hopeless failure may turn to glorious success."

Elbert Hubbard

9 Rule 6: Be Persistent and Consistent

While most rules in this book can be applied to all types of communication initiatives, not just cyber, this rule is unique because it takes input from all aspects of life to improve cyber security awareness.

This rule is focused on harnessing the human power of habit and behaviour. Generally speaking, we humans continue to do things that are easy, while we struggle with things that are more difficult.

Let's make this real—have you ever found yourself sitting in front of your TV and suddenly realize you're now on the fifth episode of your favourite show when you promised yourself that you wouldn't watch more than one episode? How did you (again) fail at maintaining discipline on reducing your TV time? Let me make you feel just a little bit better about this situation. You're not completely to blame. Blame it on human evolution. We humans have evolved to conserve energy and do the minimum necessary to make things happen. This is a smart survival strategy, and there's nothing inherently wrong with it. By auto-playing the next episode, Netflix and other streaming services like it have now required us to engage in some effort to stop the next episode! It's just more energy efficient for us to relax and keep watching. This is the power of making a behaviour so easy that we engage in it subconsciously, mostly against our best intentions.

To make another point on the connection between behaviour and perceived difficulty, let's look at a common phrase all of us have heard at some point—"An object at rest stays at rest, while an object in motion stays in motion." While this obviously relates to the laws of physics, my take on it is that we stay at rest while at rest because it's just easier that way, and we keep moving when in motion because it is—you guessed it—easier that way. Once we understand the power of getting ourselves up and moving, we must shift our focus to the next step—repetition and discipline.

Now let's explore the power of repetition to make things perfect with a quote from Michael Jordan, arguably the greatest basketball player of all time:

"I've missed more than 9,000 shots in my career. I've lost almost 300 games. Twenty-six times, I've been trusted to take the game winning shot and missed. I've failed over and over and over again in my life. And that is why I succeed."

What I love about this quote is that it beautifully sums up the power of repetition and how we humans get our best outcomes through this practice, which obviously includes an element of trial and error.

We see this happen all around us during our day-to-day interactions. I'm sure there must be plenty of research on this, but my own personal observations and conversations with the most physically-fit people I know on their secret to fitness has led to one consistent conclusion—they follow the discipline and principle of repetition. They work out most days of the week. They are human, too, so they have bad days at work, trouble with their families, and general life struggles. However, they continue the discipline through it all. Even if it's just a few push-ups and squats, they make sure to get their workout in. They may or may not realize this, but what is transforming their bodies and keeping it in good condition is the amount of repetition they are putting the body through. The idea is the same when applied to improving our brain functions. This is why I believe brain training games such as *Lumosity* require you to engage in specific actions almost every day to get results: (https://www.lumosity.com)

Talking about brain training, it is worth noting that we need to frequently revisit content to put it in our long-term memory. In 1885, German psychologist Hermann Ebbinghaus—through his famous work, *Memory: A Contribution to Experimental Psychology*—demonstrated the decrease in the ability of the brain to retain information over longer periods of time. This is now commonly referred to as the "Ebbinghaus Forgetting Curve." However, what he also discovered was that if learning is repeated at regular intervals, we forget less. He found that there is a "spacing effect" that influences how we retain information. The spacing effect refers to the phenomenon that learning is enhanced when studying is spread out over time at regular intervals, as opposed to studying the same amount of content in a single session.

The power of repetition and consistency is utilized constantly by many major organizations all over the world, such as McDonald's, who reliably delivers products and services. You should use it, too.

To summarize, when something is easy, people do it more. When people do it more, they get better at it! Let's apply these ideas to cyber security awareness efforts, which are basically all about informing and changing human behaviour.

Most cyber security awareness efforts tend to be one-off activities with no good cadence or established frequency. Some forward-looking and mature organizations have made mandatory cyber security training part of their onboarding activities, and a much smaller subset have started requiring retraining every couple of years or so. These are commendable actions, and I definitely recommend them. However, these are still not frequent enough.

I know you're probably thinking that my line of reasoning is too idealistic and there is no way you can convince either your management or users to support frequent training. Don't worry, I'm not asking you to keep going down the mandatory training path. I'm suggesting a complementary approach to training, an approach that involves short but frequent, ideally weekly, security messaging. However, the frequent messaging needs to meet these two conditions:

1. The message has to be very short, around the length of a couple of tweets.

2. It has to have a very specific action that your audience is capable of executing (e.g., a useful tip, such as how to spot malicious apps in mobile app stores like Google Play). You may provide a link to a page providing more details, but the message itself should never be bloated.

The channel for this message can be your intranet, a lunch-and-learn session, or by putting this message in a nice little cheat sheet format that managers can talk through at their weekly team meetings. If you use the approach of a cheat sheet, make sure the language is simple enough that anyone can understand. Use the principles outlined in "Rule 3 – Be SMART in Your Approach to Achieve Your Goals" and "Rule 2 – Don't Be Boring" for selecting content and communication channels. Use "Rule 5 – Harness the Power of Allies" to spread your weekly message.

Another good way to continuously reinforce content is through the adoption of the Just in Time principle, where you make quick cyber tips available to users when they're trying to do a related activity. The Just in Time training principle is based on the idea that training or learning should be provided at the time when it is needed and relevant. Some financial institutions have started using this principle rather well. For example, at the login screen of a banking website, they'll include a message saying the bank will never ask users for their passwords and to be alert to scams. The message will also include a link to a website that provides more information if users are interested. This approach works well because it provides relevant cyber reminders to users that they should never respond to any requests to share their password if they get a call or email from a scammer purporting to represent the bank, since banks will never request this under any circumstances.

An additional example of Just in Time training is when a user goes to reset their password, remind them to use a password manager to make their task easier and secure. If they want even better protection, they can use multi-factor authentication. You can then provide a link to a page that has more information on the topic. Most cyber security professionals agree that the use of multi-factor authentication, where you need an additional identifier along with the password to log into accounts, is much more secure than just using passwords. Common examples of additional identifiers used include one-time codes sent through SMS or a phone app that generates random numbers as codes.

I have personally experienced a lot of success in improving cyber security awareness through making this messaging a habit and setting a weekly cadence. For example, I introduced a concept called Cyber Thursday at a large Australian company with offices in multiple cities and thousands of employees. Every Thursday, I posted a simple cyber tip on the company's internal social networking website. Think of it as Facebook for employees. Because it was named Cyber Thursday and the tips followed the rules in this book, I started to notice high levels of engagement with the content through views, likes, and shares. I also had people come up to me and mention how they look at the website every Thursday because they'll find a new tip. By making this every Thursday and broadly socializing this term, I also keep myself honest to follow the cadence—consistency of messaging. I also keep the message and tip very simple so as to encourage action.

It's interesting how generally our attitudes seem to be chipper on Fridays and a little less enthusiastic on Monday mornings. This is obviously due to the anticipation of weekend relaxation and the less enthusiastic anticipation of the upcoming week. Hence the common phrases "Happy Friday" and "Sigh, it feels like a Monday." In my experience, the funny thing about this is that it largely holds true even if we have a relatively light workload on a Monday or have a really busy Friday. We still look forward to a Friday and don't look forward to a Monday, even on the occasional weeks when we might be working the Saturday or have a public holiday on Tuesday. Years of conditioning and habit have had this effect.

Just as people react subconsciously to Fridays and Mondays, I used a little bit of this conditioning effect for my Cyber Thursdays. You can do this, too!

The idea of consistently doing something to get better at it has spawned an entire set of mobile applications called habit tracker apps dedicated to building and reinforcing beneficial habits and actions. I have provided a link to some of these apps in the resources section.

Well-known comedian Jerry Seinfeld promotes a ritual of writing new material every day. Based on his astronomical success in the entertainment world, it'd be a safe assumption that his habit has helped him master his craft and served him quite well.

In the same way, your security messaging can work as your clients' own personal habit tracker, slowly helping them grow stronger in their cyber security awareness as they learn new skills.

To make your security awareness efforts more impactful, make them easy and do them often!

"The task of the leader is to get his people from where they are to where they have not been."

Henry Kissinger

10 Rule 7: Get the Support of Senior Leadership

I believe this is a pivotal rule, not only for cyber security awareness but for any major initiative that needs complete organizational buy-in to succeed. Following the rules in this book so far will allow you to create meaningful and engaging cyber security awareness programs. However, in order to achieve real success, you need the right tone at the top from the leadership that provides authority and support to the individual or team managing the awareness efforts.

Let's face it, there are some people in organizations—and generally all around us—on whom no amount of negotiation, persuasion, or influence will be enough to bring them to the proverbial table. In these instances, it is imperative that the security awareness program has strong executive support that articulates the non-negotiable importance of security awareness to desirable outcomes. Among the numerous awareness focus groups I've conducted, the response to one of my questions has always remained consistent. The question is, "What messages or emails do you pay the most attention to?" The context for this question is to identify the messaging channels that would work best to communicate regular awareness tips.

The most common answer to this across several industry verticals and organizations has been, "The message that comes from my manager or the C-suite."

This is precisely why I have developed the rule of getting the support of senior leadership. While it's obvious that this support is needed to ensure appropriate funding for the awareness initiatives, it also drives a lot of outcomes and behavioural changes that the activities are intending to achieve.

The most successful security awareness efforts have active participation and messaging from the top executive in the organization, such as the CEO, or in the government, such as the prime minister. I credit the success of the "Safer Internet Day 2018" effort in Australia due to a very public pledge made by then Prime Minister Hon. Malcolm Turnbull to the cause and its importance. Since all the activities of the prime minister are always heavily reported by the press and picked up by several new and old media, this simple act of making a pledge brought tremendous attention to the Safer Internet Day, and thereby all the resources and websites created to provide the public with information and tools to keep themselves and their families safe in the digital world.

Safer Internet Day is a worldwide event that has increasingly gotten people's attention in various countries thanks to similar pledges and messages made by heads of governments or the respective ministers. This shows the power of executive support.

This approach works just as well in private companies where a CEO or a member of the executive team can start a town hall meeting or send a company-wide recorded video message emphasizing the importance of cyber awareness. To make this message even more powerful, I suggest that it be more specific and tailored than just stating, "Cyber security is important." It should include a call to action and an example, such as, "Since information is the currency this digital age, and we need to protect it like we would protect our financial assets. We need all of you to make this possible by paying close attention to cyber security messages shared every month. It is incumbent upon all of us to ensure that we protect our passwords and computing devices with the care we'd take to protect our most prized physical possessions."

To ensure you achieve and continue to maintain this level of support, you need to have a clear plan on keeping the senior leadership informed of all the key cyber threats that matter and how your security awareness efforts will address them. This is no mean feat since most senior people have the busiest schedules, with multiple conflicting demands on their time. You need to be succinct, with a clear plan and requests. This is where defining objectives and measurements clearly will be very helpful. To make this happen, you should use the ideas presented in "Rule 3 – Be SMART in Your Approach."

Another suggestion I have is to make the senior leader "walk the walk." What I mean is that you should make them publicly practice some of the tips you are encouraging everyone to adopt. A good way of doing this is to leverage an existing company-wide event, such as a Q&A session with the leadership. I also see a lot of companies doing internal career development days targeted toward upward and lateral mobility of the employees. This is especially common in large companies where it would be hard for a typical employee to know the opportunities available in other lines of the business. While being an excellent employee retention mechanism, these events can serve as great platforms to reinforce awareness messaging. You can find more such events through your connections formed in "Rule 5 – Harness the Power of Allies." At these events, get the senior leader to practice one of the cyber tips. For example, get them to install a password manager and use it to demonstrate how simple and useful this tool is. Or get them to set up a PIN on their smart device for protection. You can also ask them to report a dummy suspicious email to the designated helpdesk or security contact to show how easy it is to report.

I could keep going, but you get the point. Make the leaders walk the walk. And please make sure you capture these events on video—they will be a powerful tool in your awareness promotion arsenal!

It's worth considering how we humans pay close attention to news about people in power. The spike in viewership numbers for presidential or head of government debates during election season echoes this sentiment. It's also interesting to note how people act a little differently when a senior employee walks into the room. There's an element of deference as well as greater attention paid to what is said by this person.

We should take advantage of these natural human tendencies to make our security awareness programs successful.

In summary, make certain your awareness efforts have visible support from the top-level leadership. Ensure that this support is not just paying lip-service to the cause but involves active participation. If you yourself are that senior leader in your organization, remember, you have the ability to make or break the success of security awareness programs. By choosing to read this book, I can tell you are a maker!

"Every day, every hour, this very minute, perhaps, dark forces attempt to penetrate this castle's walls. But in the end, their greatest weapon is you. Just something to think about."

Albus Dumbledore, from the movie
Harry Potter and the Half-Blood Prince

11   Coda

Culture refers to the beliefs, attitudes, behaviours, and ways of doing things among a group of people. If we apply this definition to cyber security, it would indicate that "security culture" means a set of attitudes and behaviours that promote security objectives. The thing about culture though is that it doesn't form or change overnight. It takes a lot of persistence and engagement for fundamental things like these to change.

By moving beyond ad hoc and point in time awareness activities and focusing on defining objectives aligned with establishing strategic relationships and shaping organizational behaviour, we start to move the needle toward a more holistic and secure culture. At the nirvana point of achieving true security culture, we'll have everyone in the organization recognizing and playing their part in promoting and maintaining a robust cyber security posture.

Through this book, I have shared with you a proven approach to getting cyber security awareness right. Let's quickly recap all seven rules for success.

In Rule 1, we explored the science behind why using scary news as a primary mechanism to drive behaviour is a flawed idea. Rule 2 then explained why we need to use engaging and relevant content to get our audience's attention. Applying creativity toward modes of engagement gets people interested and prevents user apathy, which is fatal for any awareness campaign. In Rule 3, we saw the importance of setting good objectives and measurements to the success of security awareness programs and also looked at clear examples and approaches toward objective and measurement definition. The rule expanded on the most important aspect of security awareness training—to motivate secure user behaviour in areas that matter the most based on business and cyber security alignment.

Rule 4 helped us understand the significance of tailoring awareness messages to different audiences, so it fits the purpose and has the best chance of succeeding in educating and training users. Rule 5 was all about achieving success through building relationships and partnerships with groups both internal and external to the organization. Rule 6 showed the power of repetition and consistency in shaping human behaviour, which leads to a more cyber-aware workforce. Rule 7 focused on the importance of senior leadership support to the success of any cyber security initiative.

In the spirit of always seeking improvement, I encourage you to keep looking for ideas and approaches from the non-cyber security world. In fact, the world of marketing is a rich source for ideas since there is a significant overlap in typical marketing objectives and the core focus of security awareness training, which is influencing people to engage in a desirable action. For example, I really like the idea of the marketing funnel, which essentially analyses the steps to get a casual observer who is aware of a product or service to become a customer.

The casual observer at the top of the marketing funnel is aware of your service but hasn't engaged much with you yet. At the centre of the funnel, the observer has learned more about your service and is actively considering a decision, so essentially, the observer now has become a potential customer. At the bottom of the funnel, the journey is complete since the customer has made the decision to buy your product or service. The model is called a funnel because there are obviously more people at the top who may be aware of your business but will not end up becoming customers.

There is value in considering a similar approach for cyber security awareness, where the first step may be casting a wide net and making everyone in your organization aware of basic security practices, then methodically focusing on changing behaviours in areas that are most meaningful, and finally getting the behaviours to stick, similar to a customer making a purchase. The seven rules in this book enable you to make that journey.

As we start to wrap this book up, I want to draw your attention to a topic that is near and dear to my heart. Earlier, we looked at various scenarios such as bad actors stealing money by compromising your accounts through phishing emails or infecting your systems with ransomware and holding your data and systems hostage until you pay them. This payment is usually demanded in cryptocurrencies such as Bitcoin. Cryptocurrencies—unlike traditional fiat currency such as dollars, pounds, and rupees—do not leave a clean money trail. This makes it really hard for law enforcement agencies to track the bad actors. While losing money and access to key information and systems is obviously devastating, the larger societal concern is also on what happens with that ransom or stolen money.

Unfortunately, a fair bit of that money ends up funding criminals who have a major role to play on the dark web, which plays host to a lot of underground marketplaces where all types of nasty things are bought and sold. Think of it as a perverse, evil version of Amazon or eBay. Every bad thing you can think of— illegal drugs, arms and ammunition, illegal pornography—is exchanged. In fact, a lot of cyber hacking tools and services are also sold on these marketplaces. It is therefore incumbent upon us to raise awareness of the value of our stolen passwords and account details and the bad actor uses of our computers and devices. By being vigilant in protecting our information and devices, we're not just helping ourselves and our organizations—we're also disrupting the scourge of the online criminal syndicate. This is the critical role that cyber security awareness plays. If you're interested in learning more on this subject, you can find a copy of my presentation on this topic at https://www.chiragdjoshi.com/.

It's also important to recognize that the advancement in technologies that has made a world with 100% online banks with no physical branches, sharing economy led by Uber and Airbnb among others, on-demand entertainment and learning, and online shopping and commerce possible relies on the trust that technology will work as it is intended to. Protecting these technologies against cyber-attacks and disruptions then should be viewed from a much larger vantage point.

Future innovations in areas such as autonomous vehicles, artificial intelligence, virtual reality, cognitive technologies, and the Internet of Things also relies on this assurance and trust in systems.

Safe and secure cyber practices will also help shape a world where the internet is a safe place for everyone, but especially for the most vulnerable amongst us, including kids and seniors.

I'll conclude with a personal story:

I spent my early years growing up in India before moving to the United States for my education. I still have a lot of family and childhood friends in Mumbai, whom I visit often.

India is a fascinating country, with a population of over a billion people, multiple religions, and over 100 different active languages! It is an amazingly diverse country, both geographically and demographically. The one constant in India's quick rise as a regional powerhouse has been its democracy. Despite all its internal differences, India has a strong and vibrant democracy where elections are held every five years for a peaceful transfer of power. The common citizens of the country believe in the system and the power of their vote to change governments. While this is common in most of the western world, it is still rare in southeast Asia. The trust in the system of elections and democracy is a foundational element of India's existence and progress as one united country.

Being the world's largest democracy, it naturally holds the world's largest elections. Because of the size of the population, voting doesn't happen simultaneously nationwide in one day. It happens over a period of a few weeks in multiple phases.

Now, I've always had a lot of interest in politics, both local and global. As a kid, I used to keenly watch the election coverage and the results with my dad. I loved watching the counts come in with all the excitement, seesawing numbers, fancy charts, and predictions! While elections were generally peaceful and reliable, you always had pockets of criminal behaviour called "booth capturing." Basically, it was a bunch of criminals taking over a polling station and tampering with the paper ballots to change the outcome to their benefactors, who were corrupt politicians. This was a stain on democracy and a mockery of the election process. It also ensured the presence of heavily-corrupt elements in the government legislatures.

Around the late 1990s though, a very interesting change occurred. India started replacing paper ballots with Electronic Voting Machines (EVMs). This and the accompanying improvement in policing played a transformational role in bringing complete integrity to the election process. These EVMs took away the issues of paper ballot tampering, which helped reduce corruption in politics. Democracy and the vote of the people were the big winners. It also made the reporting process much more efficient since results were now declared within a couple of days as opposed to the weeks it took with paper ballots.

Now, the entire premise of using EVMs is based on a simple idea of trust in the digital system. It is that trust and assurance that the EVMs are capturing every vote accurately and irreversibly that causes people to believe in the system. Unfortunately, in the last few years, losing political parties have started floating the idea that these machines may be hacked. This is a cynical move playing on people's lack of understanding of how technology works and taking advantage of all the negative global news around cyber security. Some politicians have even suggested bringing back paper processes altogether. This suits their narrow purpose because they can go back to the old, dark days of booth capturing but is an obviously terrible outcome for the common citizen.

This is what is at stake when it comes to promoting trust in technology and making people aware of real cyber security risks. The new digital world, which affords us so much convenience, progress, and advancements in all aspects of life, will not function without foundational trust in digital information and systems. This is the real value of cyber security and, consequently, the importance of cyber security awareness.

I want to express my deep gratitude to you for reading this book, and I sincerely hope you were able to get something out of the time you invested in it. I hope this is not the end of our conversation. I'd love to connect with you on LinkedIn, and please feel free to contact me through my website:

https://www.chiragdjoshi.com.

I want to request a favour from you. If you've enjoyed this book, please post a review expressing how you liked it on the platform where you purchased it. For authors such as myself, nothing means more than kind words from those who we strive to provide value to through our writing. I'd also love to hear stories of the experiences you've had in implementing these rules!

12   References and Additional Resources

References

Chowdhury, R., Sharot, T., Wolfe, T., Düzel, E., &
Dolan, R. J. (2014). Optimistic update bias
increases in older age. Psychological medicine,
44(9), 2003–2012.
doi:10.1017/S0033291713002602

Fazzini, Kate. 2019. "Google and Facebook Got
Tricked Out of $123 Million by a Scam That
Costs Small Businesses Billions Every Year—
Here's How to Avoid It." *CNBC*, March 28,
2019. https://www.cnbc.com/2019/03/28/how-
to-avoid-invoice-theft-scam-that-cost-google-
facebook-123m.html

Fellner, Carrie. 2019. "Australian Catholic University
staff details stolen in fresh data breach." *The
Sydney Morning Herald,* June 17, 2019.
https://www.smh.com.au/national/australian-
catholic-university-staff-details-stolen-in-fresh-
data-breach-20190617-p51yif.html

Mendonca, Jochelle. 2019. "Wipro Confirms Attack on IT Systems, Hires Forensic Investigation Firm." *Economic Times*, April 17, 2019. https://tech.economictimes.indiatimes.com/news /corporate/wipro-it-systems-may-have-been-hacked-and-used-to-attack-its-clients-report/68899479

Moutsiana, C., Garrett, N., Clarke, R. C., Lotto, R. B., Blakemore, S. J., & Sharot, T. (2013). Human development of the ability to learn from bad news. Proceedings of the National Academy of Sciences of the United States of America, 110(41), 16396–16401. doi:10.1073/pnas.1305631110

TEDx Talks. 2014. "How to motivate yourself to change your behavior | Tali Sharot | TEDxCambridge." *YouTube video*, 16:48. Posted October 28, 2014. https://www.youtube.com/watch?v=xp0O2vi8D X4

UK Government Cabinet Office and Behavioural Insights Team. 2012. "Applying behavioural

insights to reduce fraud, error and debt."
Gov.UK, February 6, 2012.
https://assets.publishing.service.gov.uk/governm
ent/uploads/system/uploads/attachment_data/file
/60539/BIT_FraudErrorDebt_accessible.pdf

Verizon. 2019. "2019 Data Breach Investigations
Report." https://enterprise.verizon.com/en-
au/resources/reports/dbir/

Waters, S. F., West, T. V., Karnilowicz, H. R., &
Mendes, W. B. (2017). Affect contagion
between mothers and infants: Examining
valence and touch. Journal of experimental
psychology. General, 146(7), 1043–1051.
doi:10.1037/xge0000322

Additional Resources

The latest version of this list is available on https://www.chiragdjoshi.com/.

Websites with Free Cyber Security Awareness Content:

- SANS Ouch Security Awareness newsletters: https://www.sans.org/security-awareness-training/ouch-newsletter
- https://www.staysmartonline.gov.au/
- https://www.getsafeonline.org/
- https://www.esafety.gov.au/
- https://www.scamwatch.gov.au
- https://www.ic3.gov/preventiontips.aspx
- https://www.knowbe4.com/free-it-security-tools
- https://theanalogiesproject.org/

Websites for Cyber Security News and Information:

- https://www.krebsonsecurity.com
- https://www.theregister.co.uk/security/
- https://thecyberwire.com/index.html

Cyber Risk:

- https://nvlpubs.nist.gov/nistpubs/legacy/sp/nistspecialpublication800-30r1.pdf
- http://www.isaca.org/Knowledge-Center/Research/ResearchDeliverables/Pages/The-Risk-IT-Framework.aspx
- https://www.nist.gov/cyberframework

Password Managers:

- Last Pass: https://www.lastpass.com/password-manager
- KeePass: https://keepass.info/

Phishing Simulations:

- Open source: https://resources.infosecinstitute.com/top-9-free-phishing-simulators/

- Cofense PhishMe:
https://cofense.com/product-services/phishme/

- Wombat:
https://www.wombatsecurity.com/security-education/simulated-phishing-and-knowledge-assessments

Professional Associations:

- ISACA: https://www.isaca.org
- AISA: https://www.aisa.org.au
- ISC2: https://www.isc2.org/
- OWASP: https://www.owasp.org
- Cloud Security Alliance:
https://www.cloudsecurityalliance.org

Habit Tracker Apps Link:

- https://www.lifehack.org/668261/best-habit-tracking-apps

More About the Wipro Incident:

- https://www.itnews.com.au/news/wipro-hacked-internal-systems-used-to-attack-customers-report-523956

- https://krebsonsecurity.com/2019/04/how-not-to-acknowledge-a-data-breach/

Book on learning more about how the human brain works and approaches influencing others:

- *The Influential Mind: What the Brain Reveals About Our Power to Change Others* by Tali Sharot

13   About the Author

Chirag's ambitious goal is simple—to enable human progress through technology. To accomplish this, he wants to help build a world where there is trust in digital systems, protection against cyber threats, and a safe environment online for communication, commerce, and engagement. He is especially passionate about the safety of children and vulnerable sections of society online. This goal has served as a motivation that has led Chirag to become a sought-after speaker and advocate at various industry-leading conferences and events across multiple countries.

Chirag has extensive experience working directly with the C-suite executives to implement cyber security awareness training programs in Australia and the United States. During the course of his career spanning over a decade across multiple sectors, he has built, implemented, and successfully managed cyber security, risk management, and compliance programs. The success of these programs was a result of unyielding focus on business priorities, a pragmatic approach to cyber threats, and most importantly, effective stakeholder engagement. As a leader holding senior positions in organizations, Chirag excels at the art of translating business and technical speak in a manner that optimizes value.

Chirag has also conducted several successful cyber training and awareness sessions for non-technical audiences in diverse industries such as finance, energy, healthcare, and higher education.

Chirag's academic qualifications include a master's degree in telecommunications management from Oklahoma State University and a bachelor's degree in electronics and telecommunications engineering from the University of Mumbai. He holds multiple certifications, including Certified Information Security Manager, Certified Information Systems Auditor, and Certified in Risk and Information Systems Control.

His areas of expertise include executive cyber and technology governance, cyber risk management, security awareness training, and cloud computing.

© Chirag D Joshi, 2019

All Rights Reserved

Printed in February 2023
by Rotomail Italia S.p.A., Vignate (MI) - Italy